PATTERN MAGIC STRETCH FABRICS

Tomoko Nakamichi

Laurence King Publishing

LAURENCE KING

Published in 2012 by Laurence King Publishing Ltd

361–373 City Road

London EC1V 1LR

United Kingdom

Tel: + 44 20 7841 6900

Fax: + 44 20 7841 6910

e-mail: enquiries@laurenceking.com

www.laurenceking.com

Pattern Magic: Stretch Fabrics by Tomoko Nakamichi

Copyright © Tomoko Nakamichi 2010

Original Japanese edition published by EDUCATIONAL FOUNDATION BUNKA GAKUEN BUNKA PUBLISHING BUREAU.

This English edition is published by arrangement with EDUCATIONAL FOUNDATION BUNKA GAKUEN BUNKA PUBLISHING BUREAU, Tokyo, in care of Tuttle-Mori Agency, Inc., Tokyo.

Tomoko Nakamichi has asserted her right under the Copyright, Designs, and Patent Act 1988, to be identified as the Author of this Work.

A catalogue record for this book is available from the British Library.

ISBN: 978-1-85669-827-6

Original publisher: Sunao Onuma

Original design and layout: Tomoko Okayama

Photography: Masaaki Kawada

Original editor: Yukiko Miyazaki (BUNKA PUBLISHING BUREAU)

Translated from the Japanese by Andy Walker

Technical consultant for translation: Chika Ito

English edition design and typesetting: Mark Holt

Senior Editor: Sophie Wise

Typeface: Sabon and Syntax

Printed in China

Tomoko Nakamichi

Having served for many years as a professor at Bunka Fashion College, Tomoko Nakamichi currently delivers lectures and holds courses on pattern making in her native Japan and internationally.

This book brings together the results of the research on garment patterns she has carried out to help her instruct her students.

She is also the author of *Pattern Magic* and *Pattern Magic 2*.

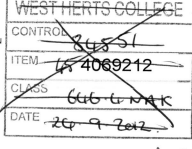

PATTERN MAGIC
STRETCH FABRICS

A garment in stretch fabric can be anything your body makes it.

Once you put your arms through, the fabric adapts freely to emphasize your silhouette.

This book, then, is as much about wearing garments as about exalting the merits of making them.

It is about garments that offer a sense of freedom beyond the scribbles and calculations that we do in our minds.

Interpreting garments that take shape as if by magic is fun and just like playing a game.

Contents

The magic is in the wearing
20...........40

Using this book
8

Part 1
Fun with stretch fabrics

Wear it wrong
11............30

Two peas in a pod A
12............32

Two peas in a pod B
14............34

Full moon
16, 18............36

Crescent moon
17, 19............38

Whac-A-Mole
22............42

Hooded shirt
24............44

Pattern mystery
26............46

Crushed can
28............47

Part 2
The expressive power of stretch fabrics

Roots A
49............70

Roots B
49............72

 Sharp and snappy A
50............74

Sharp and snappy B
51............75

Sharp and snappy C
52............76

 Sharp and snappy D
53............78

 Apple peel A
54............79

 Apple peel B
56............80

 Jutting edge
58............82

 Circular drape
59............84

 Stopper
60............86

 Loophole A
62............88

 Loophole B
62............90

 Straight lines and
curves A
64............93

 Straight lines and
curves B
65............94

 Kangaroo
66............96

Stingray
68............100

Enlarging and reducing patterns
102

Using this book

Most of the pieces in this book use a "sloper" (block)—see its characteristics below—but the patterns will produce garments with a neat fit provided you make them with material that is reasonably stretchy.

The pattern drafting and manipulations for the garment designs in this book are based on the sloper for women of Japanese 'M' size (bust 83cm, waist 64cm, hips 91cm, back length 38cm, and sleeve length 52cm), and a half-scale dress form for three-dimensional pattern manipulation. All the measurements on this dress form are half that of a full-sized dress form; its surface area is scaled down to a quarter, and its volume to one eighth.

Although the variation in the thickness and hang of the material can make the balance of the garment appear different from when it is produced at full size, using a half-scale dress form has the advantage of making it easier to appreciate the overall balance and mood of a garment.

I have also opted to provide a method of learning how patterns work that has the convenience of using smaller amounts of fabric and taking less time. When drafting a pattern at half-scale, remember to halve all of the numbers in the pattern drawing as well.

As my objective was to explain the construction of a pattern in an easy-to-follow way, I have omitted pattern markings such as the facing lines used for actually constructing the garment and the amount of fabric required to make the garment in practice.

● You will find full- and half-size patterns for the sloper (block) (in S, M, and L sizes) at the back of this book. You simply have to choose the right one for your purpose.

Characteristics of the slopers (blocks) used

The major difference with slopers used for non-stretch fabrics is that the pattern is designed to fit closely to the body. The parts of the pattern that are distinctive are as follows:

- The shoulders are narrowed such that the sleeve folds onto the shoulder.
- The bottom arm hole is raised and the arm hole reduced in size.
- The sleeves are also narrowed to fit the arms.
- The arm holes and sleeve caps are the same measurement.
- The hips are smaller than the actual measurements to produce a close fit.
- The waist curve is drawn almost as a straight line to fit the body.
- The neckline is opened out significantly to allow the garment to be pulled on.

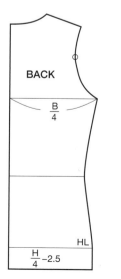

BACK

$\dfrac{B}{4}$

HL

$\dfrac{H}{4} - 2.5$

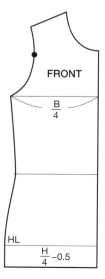

FRONT

$\dfrac{B}{4}$

HL

$\dfrac{H}{4} - 0.5$

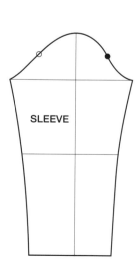

SLEEVE

Materials used

Stretch fabrics include plain knit, circular rib, double rib, and rib stitch fabric. Circular rib and rib stitch are good at stretching horizontally, while materials that contain polyurethane will stretch vertically too. For the slopers (blocks), I have used a bare plain knit, which is a cotton fabric mixed with polyurethane and other components. It stretches well, but does curl, so I would use something nice and stretchy like circular rib or rib stitch if this is a problem.

The photographs show the bare plain knit that I have used for the slopers being stretched with normal force. Many of the pieces in this book use an easily stretchable material like a bare plain knit to give a fitted feel to the garment.

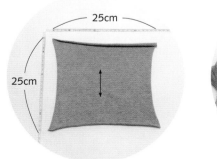
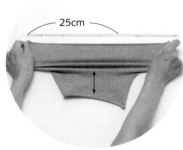
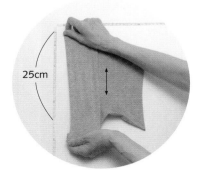

Symbols and abbreviations used in pattern drafting

Abbreviations used in pattern drafting

AH
Arm Hole

FAH
Front Arm Hole

BAH
Back Arm Hole

B
Bust

W
Waist

H
Hip

BL
Bust Line

WL
Waist Line

HL
Hip Line

EL
Elbow Line

CF
Center Front

CB
Center Back

Symbols used in pattern drafting

Guide line		Line that acts as a guide when drawing other lines. Shown by a thin solid line.
Sector line		Line indicating that one line of a fixed length has been divided into equal lengths. Shown by a thin broken line.
Finishing line		Line indicating the finished outline of a pattern. Shown by a thick solid line or a broken line.
Cut on the fold		Line indicating where the fabric is to be cut on the fold. Shown by a thick broken line.
Right angle marking		Indicates a right angle. Shown by a thin solid line.
Line intersection		Indicates an intersection of the lines on the left and right.
Grain line		Indicates that the cross-wise grain of the fabric runs in the direction of the arrow. Shown by a thick solid line.
Bias direction		Indicates the direction of the bias of the fabric. Shown by a thick solid line.
Cut open marking		Indicates that the paper pattern is to be cut open.
Cutting out the fabric with one piece pattern		Indicates that the paper pattern pieces are to be arranged contiguously when cutting out the fabric.

Part 1
Fun with stretch fabrics

Material that stretches back and forth freely is already suffused with magic.

It expands and contracts cross-wise, length-wise, and diagonally to fit the body, transforming with ease to create beautiful draped effects.

It's no exaggeration to say that the garment requires nothing more than to be put on.

Discovering a flexible pattern especially intended for this material opens up the possibility of designs that are impossible to achieve with non-stretch fabrics.

Let's take a look at how to turn that freedom into a pattern by applying it to a garment definition.

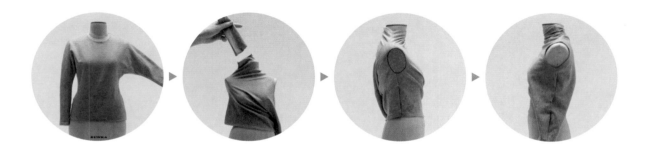

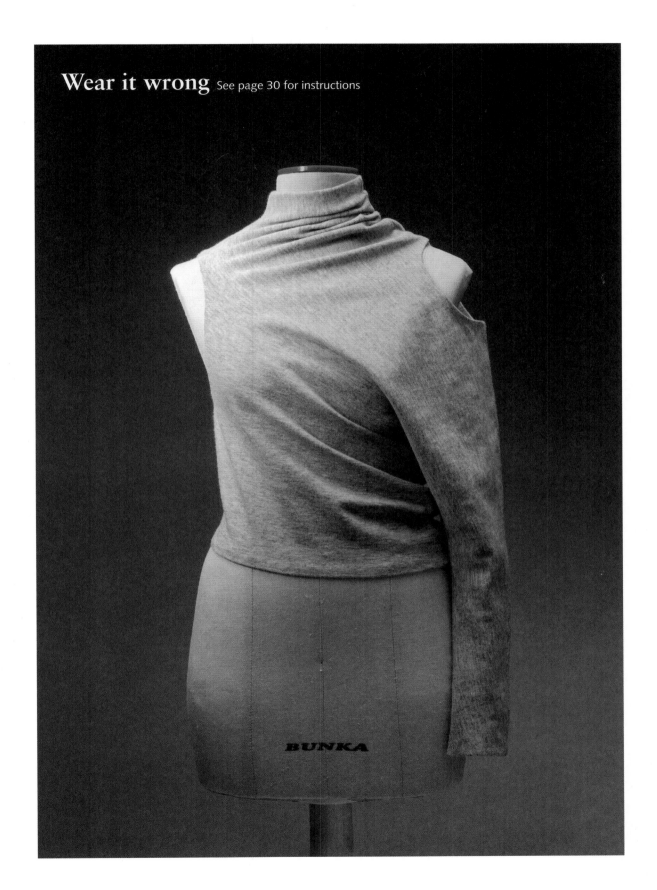

Wear it wrong See page 30 for instructions

Two peas in a pod A See page 32 for instructions

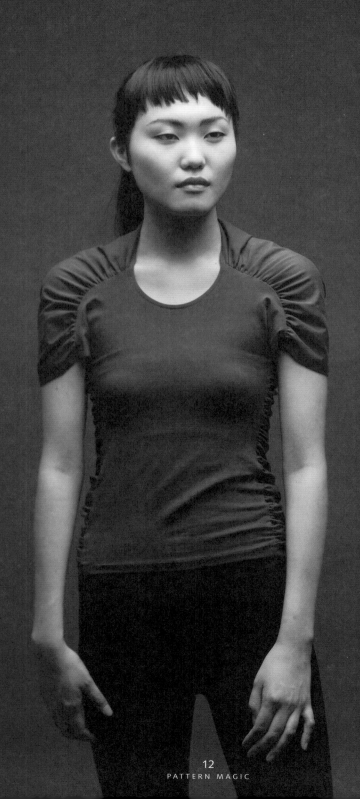

Full moon See page 36 for instructions

Crescent moon See page 38 for instructions

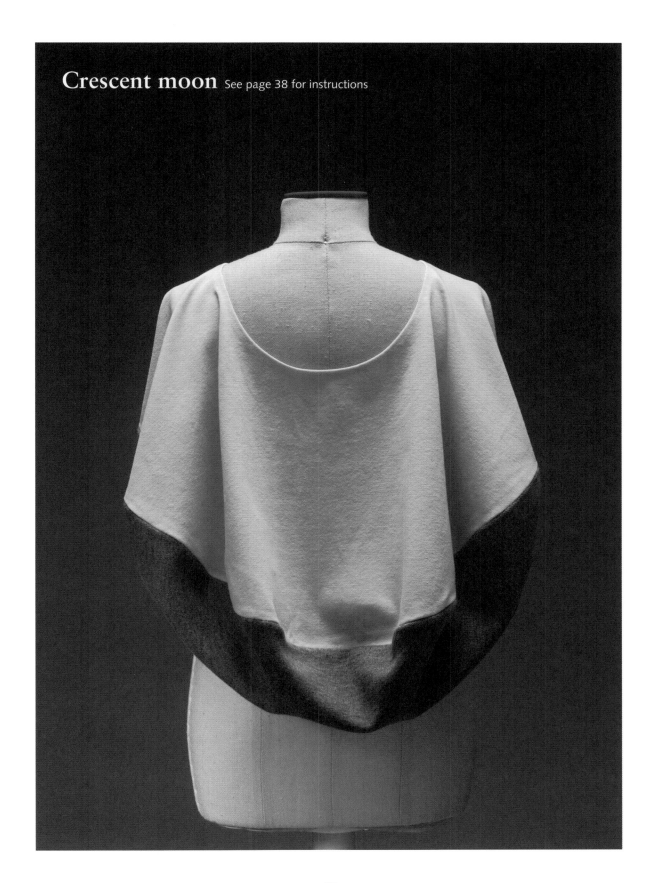

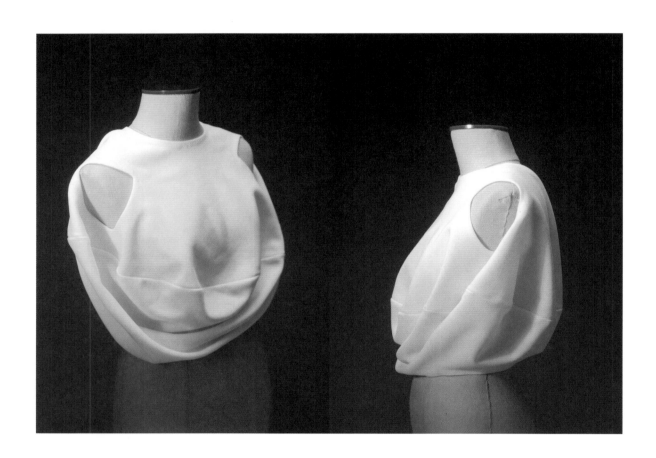

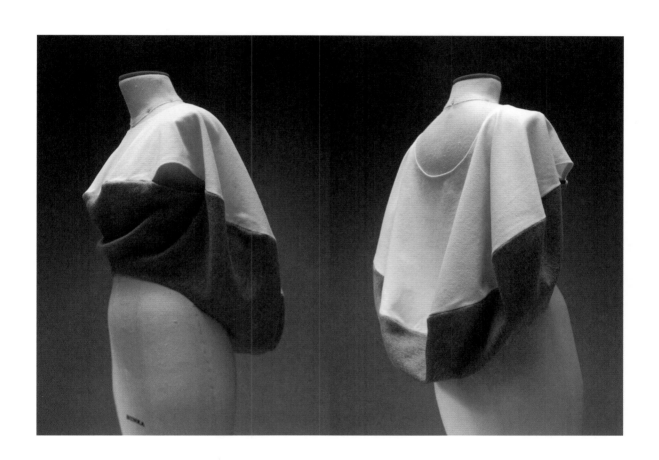

The magic is in the wearing See page 40 for instructions

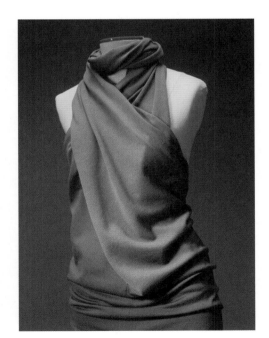

21

Whac-A-Mole See page 42 for instructions

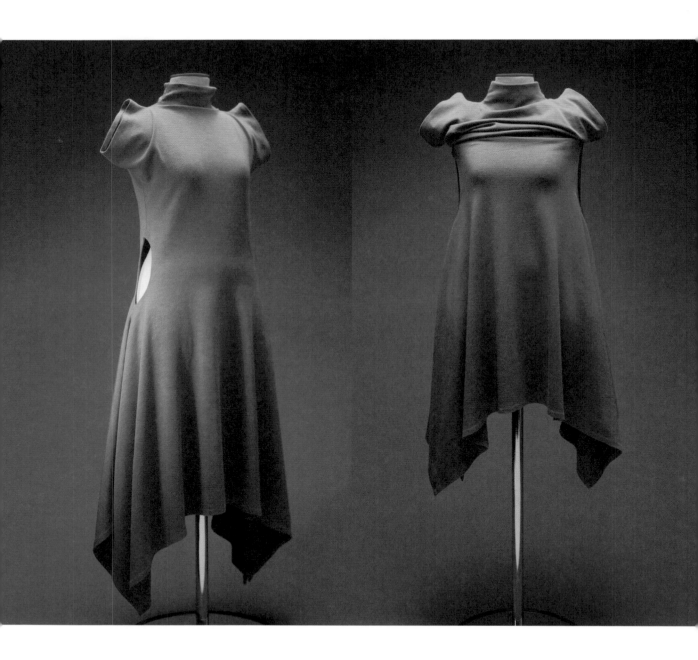

23

Hooded shirt See page 44 for instructions

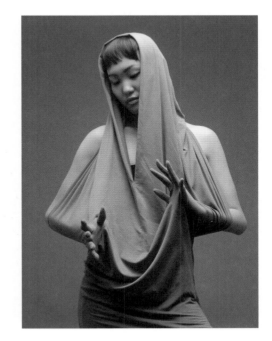

Crushed can See page 47 for instructions

Making the patterns for
Fun with stretch fabrics

Page 11: Wear it wrong

We all have those mornings when we're running late,
doing our buttons up wrong in a panic,
trying to get our head through the sleeve...
And yet, putting things on the wrong way
can make for some interesting results.
Here, we'll remodel a kimono-sleeve shirt
into a more avant-garde design.

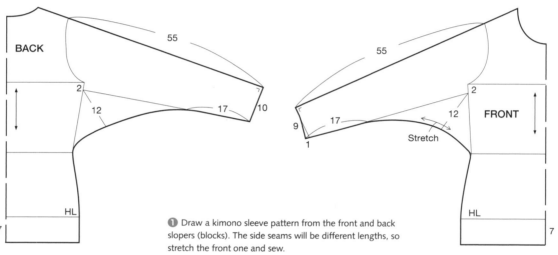

❶ Draw a kimono sleeve pattern from the front and back slopers (blocks). The side seams will be different lengths, so stretch the front one and sew.

❷ Put the finished kimono-sleeve shirt on the dress form.

❸ Pull the right sleeve over the head. The neckline comes over the left shoulder, creating a sleeveless effect. The garment also hangs out at the right side.

❹ Check that there is enough width for the head to go through, and trim off the excess sleeve. The sleeve turns into a high neck.

❺ Pin the protruding right side.

The remade pattern

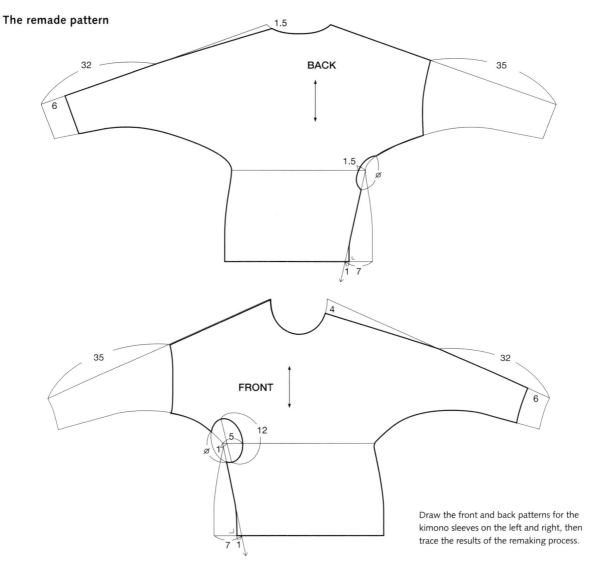

BACK

1.5

32

35

6

1.5

1 7

FRONT

4

35

32

6

5 12

7 1

Draw the front and back patterns for the
kimono sleeves on the left and right, then
trace the results of the remaking process.

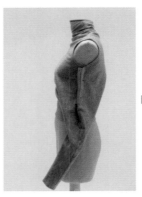

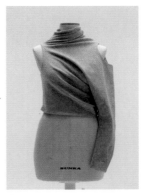

6 Arrange the right side, taping
at the position that will form the
neckline. Cut gradually to size,
bearing in mind that the neckline
will stretch easily.

7 The left sleeve is too wide and
the shoulder hole too large. To
make the left sleeve look neater,
pin and then narrow the width of
the sleeve.

8 Arrange the left sleeve,
shortening the sleeve length.

9 Sew up to complete.

Page 12: Two peas in a pod A

I combined a little shirt with a big one
to produce something of standard size.

The two of them hit it off like two peas in a pod.

Use a copier to enlarge and reduce the pattern. Alternatively,
you can use the method on page 102.

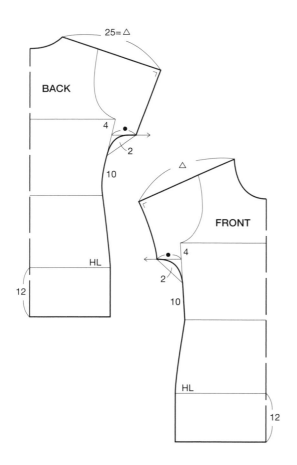

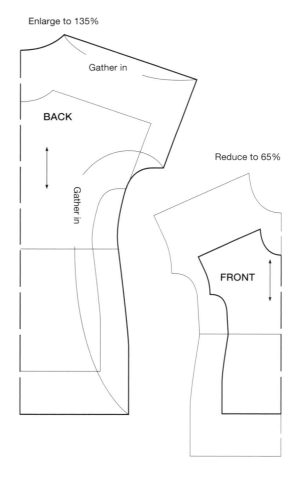

❶ Draw up from the hip line on the front and back slopers (blocks)
and draw the pattern for the kimono sleeve.

❷ Enlarge the bodice back to 135% and copy. Reduce the bodice
front to 65% and copy. Gather the sides and shoulders of the back and
sew onto the front.

Page 14: Two peas in a pod B

Like someone assembling toy building blocks,
I combined large and small T-shaped patterns in
reverse directions, which was all it took to produce
a blouse with a folk flavor.

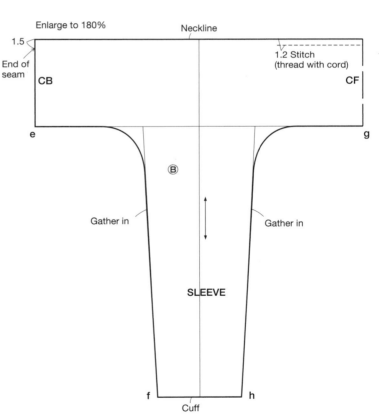

Finished drawing

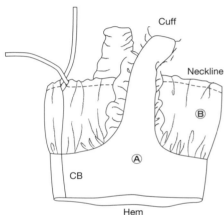

Cord   160   0.7

Enlarge to 180%

1.5

End of seam

CB   Neckline   1.2 Stitch (thread with cord)   CF

e   g

Ⓑ

Gather in   Gather in

SLEEVE

f   Cuff   h

Cuff

5.5 / 5.5

b   d

SLEEVE

37

Ⓐ

a   2.5   2.5   c

7.5 / 7.5

CB   12   CF

22   Hem   22

❶ Draw the pattern for the upside-down T-shape with the bodice below the bust joined to the under sleeve, marking it as Ⓐ.

❷ To make the pattern with the bodice above the bust joined to the outer sleeve, enlarge Ⓐ to 180%, turn upside down, and mark as Ⓑ. Sew together a-b and e-f, and c-d and g-h. Thread the neckline with the drawstring and adjust.

Page 16: Full moon

The moon only ever faces us from the front,
and so reveals the same patterns from anywhere
on earth, a rabbit, say, or a woman's face in profile...

A full moon made by sewing together two circles
can be turned into garments with differing
expressions by changing the position
of the neckline and arm holes.

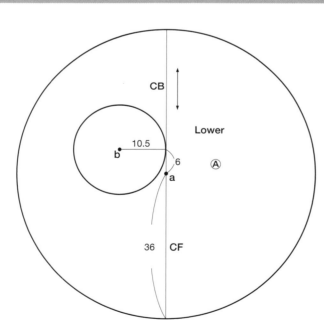

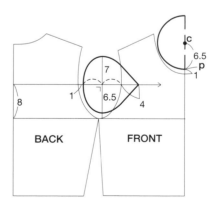

❶ Draw a circle of radius 36cm around a. Inside that circle, draw another circle of radius 10.5cm around b for the waist. Check that the bust will fit through, as the garment will be put on through the waist. Mark as circle Ⓐ, which will be the lower face of the garment.

❷ Draw the pattern for the arm holes and neckline. Draw the arm hole by aligning the point of the sleeve bottom from above the waist on the front and back slopers (blocks). Draw a circle of radius 6.5cm around point c on the center front line to make the neckline.

3 Make a circle Ⓑ the same size as Ⓐ but without the holes in it. Ⓑ will be the topmost circle when the garment is worn. Sew Ⓐ and Ⓑ together.

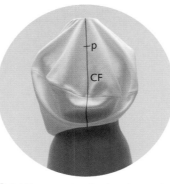

4 Put the garment on the dress form and move it around until you find the desired silhouette. Mark the center front line at the front neck point, p.

5 The back is pulled up by neck of the dress form.

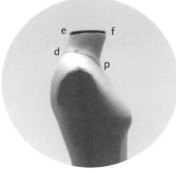

6 Make the length of the dress form's neck (d-e-f-p) that of △.

7 Lower the bodice back by the distance represented by △ and check the silhouette. If the silhouette is not to your liking, go back to step **4** and repeat the procedure.

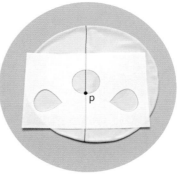

8 Lie the pattern flat with Ⓑ on top. Align the pattern produced in **2** with the center front and p, and set in place. Trace the neckline and arm holes onto the bodice.

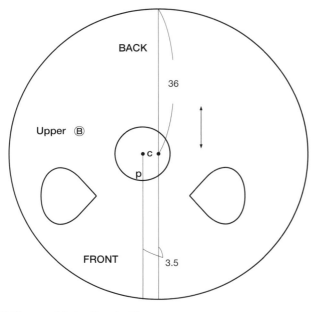

BACK

36

Upper Ⓑ

c

p

FRONT

3.5

9 The completed pattern for Ⓑ.

Page 17: Crescent moon

The moon waxes and wanes constantly, forever changing its shape.

With a moon made of fabric, two pieces of material of different colors produce an ethereal crescent shape on the back.

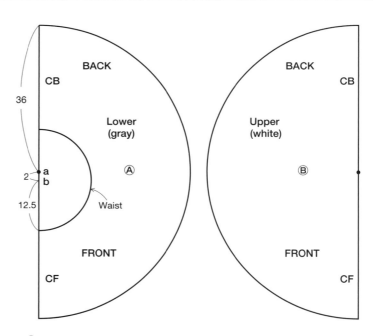

❶ Draw a circle of radius 36cm around a. Inside that circle, draw another circle of radius 12.5cm around b for the waist. This will form the lower circle Ⓐ. Make a circle Ⓑ that is as circle Ⓐ but without the hole. Ⓑ will form the upper circle.

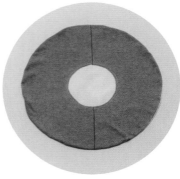

❷ Sew Ⓐ and Ⓑ together and place on the dress form.

❸ Move the garment around until you find the right silhouette. Mark the center front line and the front neck point, p.

❹ Cut out a circle big enough for the neck of the dress form to pass through p and slide the garment onto the dress form.

❺ Mark the neckline by taping along the desired line.

❻ Mark the armhole using the seam line to open for sleeves.

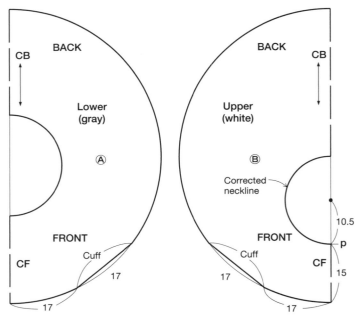

❼ To complete the pattern, trace and draw the neckline and cuffs onto Ⓐ and Ⓑ.

Page 20: The magic is in the wearing

From a rectangle of fabric imbued with magic to a sophisticated, bare-shouldered look.

By twisting, unfolding, knotting, and threading, the garment can be worn in any number of ways, to which the wearer adds her own magic.

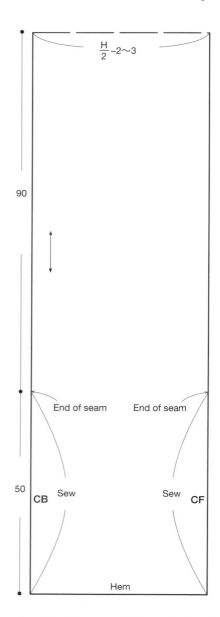

$\frac{H}{2} - 2 \sim 3$

90

End of seam   End of seam

50 CB Sew   Sew CF

Hem

Draw the pattern. The garment will be worn fitted at the hips, so reduce the amount of ease.

Page 22: Whac-A-Mole

A dress with the head emerging in different places is like a Whac-A-Mole game in which the head keeps popping out no matter how many times you bash it.

The exhilaration of whacking the mole might be missing, but the fun here is to see the silhouette change whenever you make the head or arms come out of a different hole.

Put the head through the high-neck in the middle. Put the arms through the high-necks on either side. This creates a slightly draped effect under the sleeves and produces a long dress with a hole at the sides.

Put the head through the high-neck in the middle. Pass the arms through the holes in the side. The high-necks pushed up onto the shoulders at either side bring out the square-shouldered silhouette, producing a draped effect over the chest.

Put the head through the high-neck on the left. Pass the arms through the holes in the side. This creates an asymmetrical look, with the remaining high-neck pushed up onto the shoulder , giving an avant-garde feel in combination with the draped feature on the chest.

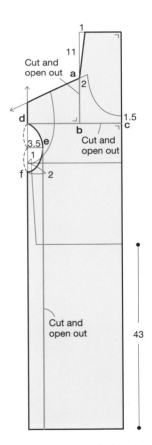

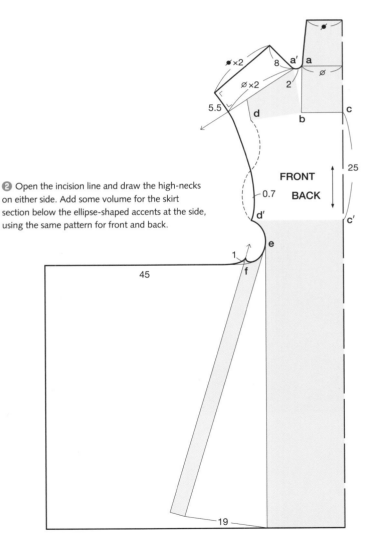

❷ Open the incision line and draw the high-necks on either side. Add some volume for the skirt section below the ellipse-shaped accents at the side, using the same pattern for front and back.

❶ Draw up from the waist on the front sloper (block). Draw the high-neck in the middle and add the incision lines for the high-necks on either side. Determine the dress length. On the side lines, cut an ellipse-shaped hole for the arm holes that will also form an accent. Draw the incision lines out from the hole.

Page 24: Hooded shirt

Which plays the starring role, the hood, or the shirt?

Pulling on a hood integrated with a shirt has a certain humorous quality, like that of a Daruma doll.

Take the hood off, and it turns into a baggy collar at the back.

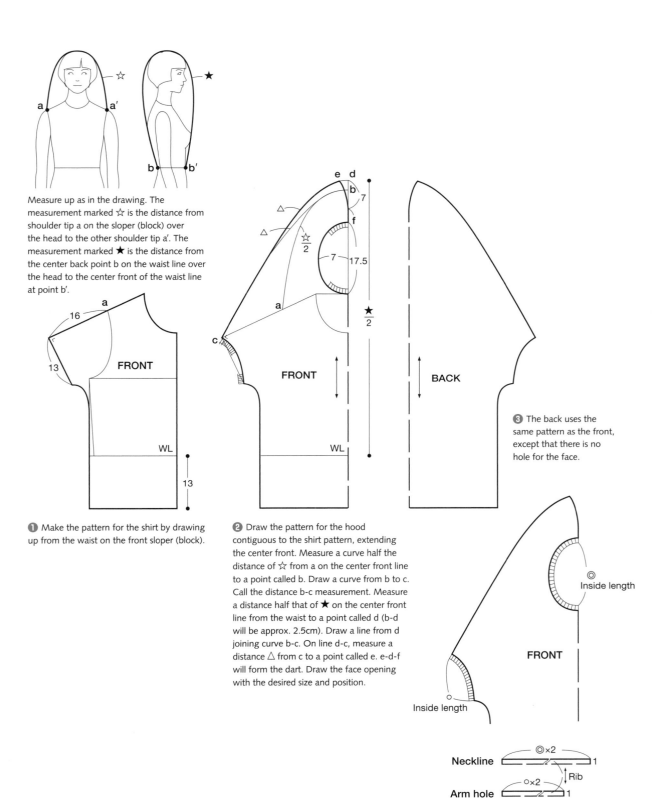

Measure up as in the drawing. The measurement marked ☆ is the distance from shoulder tip a on the sloper (block) over the head to the other shoulder tip a'. The measurement marked ★ is the distance from the center back point b on the waist line over the head to the center front of the waist line at point b'.

❶ Make the pattern for the shirt by drawing up from the waist on the front sloper (block).

❷ Draw the pattern for the hood contiguous to the shirt pattern, extending the center front. Measure a curve half the distance of ☆ from a on the center front line to a point called b. Draw a curve from b to c. Call the distance b-c measurement. Measure a distance half that of ★ on the center front line from the waist to a point called d (b-d will be approx. 2.5cm). Draw a line from d joining curve b-c. On line d-c, measure a distance △ from c to a point called e. e-d-f will form the dart. Draw the face opening with the desired size and position.

❸ The back uses the same pattern as the front, except that there is no hole for the face.

Inside length

Inside length

FRONT

Neckline	◎×2	1
Arm hole	○×2	1

Rib

❹ Add ribs to the cuffs and hood opening. Set the rib length to be the inside measurement.

Page 26: Pattern mystery

What if there were fingers sprouting from a flat piece of fabric, and then those fingers started to move...?

Mysterious events do not belong only in books and movies, as our pattern mystery emerging from a simple rectangle of fabric proves.

① Trace round the shape of your hand.

② Cut at the point where the hand will look realistic.

③ Smoothly and continuously draw in an outside margin of 0.3cm to give wearing ease for the fingers.

④ We will use the design lines to bring out the hand, so add vertical design lines to the rectangle and divide it into three parts. Draw in the traced hand and the seam end.

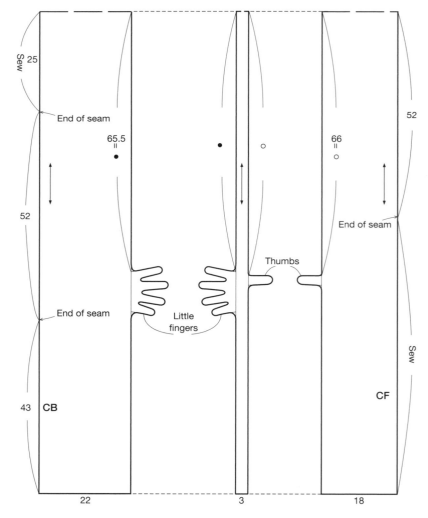

Page 28: Crushed can

Bringing in a long tube top gives it the draped effect of a crushed can.

With non-stretch materials, you would require tailoring skills to pull this off, but stretch materials need no such attention.

We'll also add triangles to the sides to create edges when the piece is crushed down.

The more you crush, the sharper the edges.

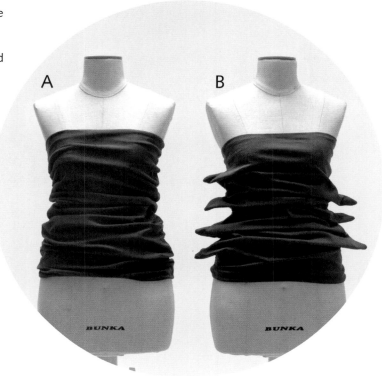

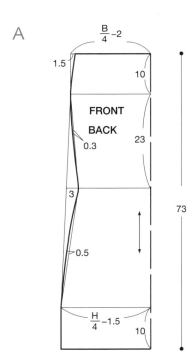

A

$\frac{B}{4} - 2$

1.5

10

FRONT

BACK

0.3

23

3

73

0.5

$\frac{H}{4} - 1.5$

10

Draw the pattern for the bodice. To ensure that the garment fits, allow more space for the bust and hips, using the same pattern for front and back.

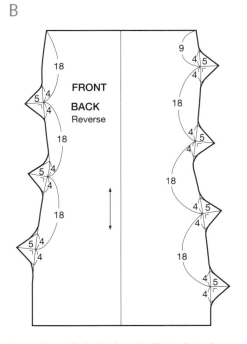

B

9

4 5

18

4

FRONT

5 4

BACK
Reverse

18

4

18

5 4

4

18

4 5

4

18

4

18

5 4

4

4 5

4

Draw pattern A for both sides and add triangles to the sides. Turn the pattern over for the back.

Part 2
The expressive power of stretch fabrics

Making a piece of clothing is always exciting.

Ideas come to me from everywhere.

It might be something that I've read or that touched me on my travels,
a word that I've heard someone say, or a memory from my childhood...

And it's thrilling to see such things take shape from fabric, turning into
different garments.

Garments made from stretch materials have a softly expressive quality
that adapts itself to the heart and mind of the person creating them.

Transforming a freely expressed three-dimensional shape into a
two-dimensional pattern gives me the same sense of achievement as
solving a puzzle.

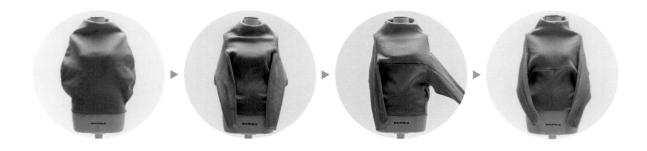

Roots See page 70 for instructions

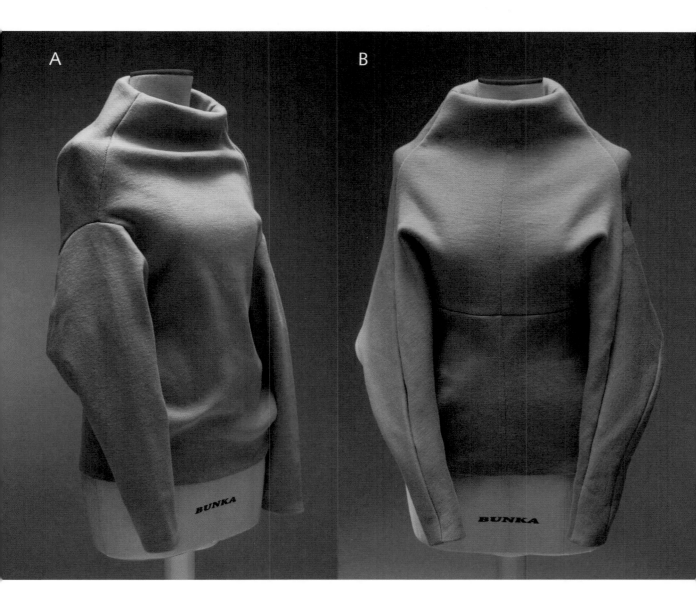

A

B

Sharp and snappy A See page 74 for instructions

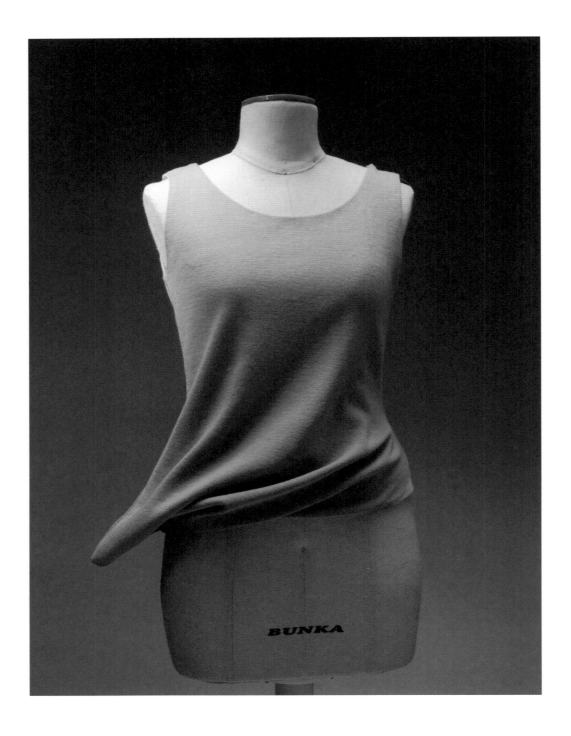

Sharp and snappy B See page 75 for instructions

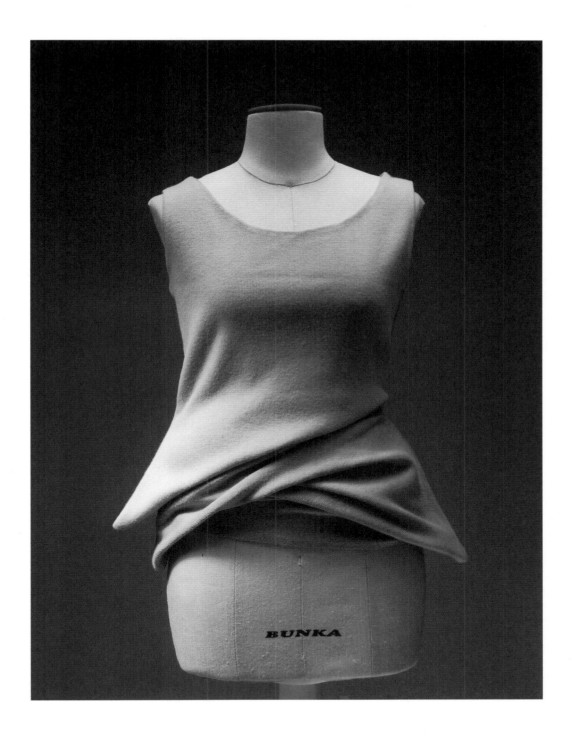

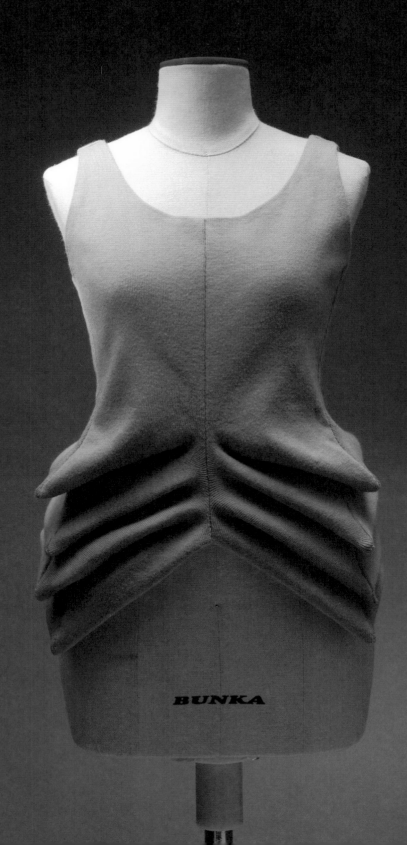

Sharp and snappy D See page 78 for instructions

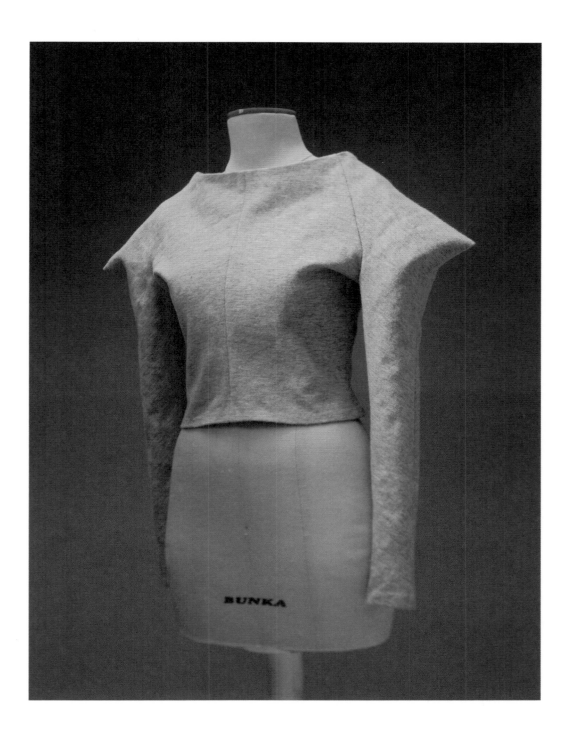

Apple peel A See page 79 for instructions

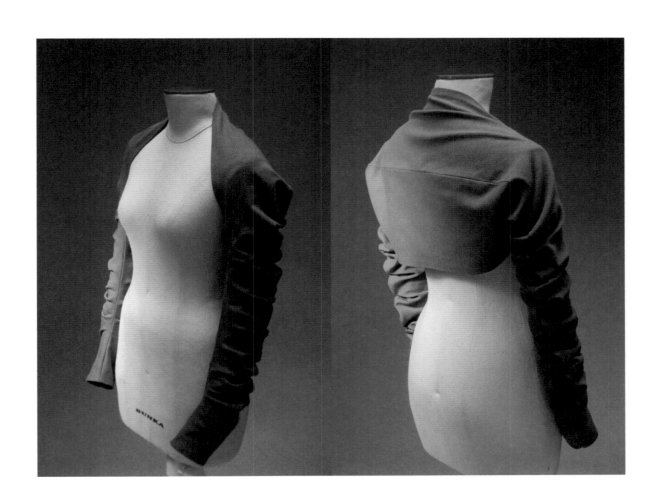

Apple peel B See page 80 for instructions

Jutting edge See page 82 for instructions

Circular drape design See page 84 for instructions

Stopper See page 86 for instructions

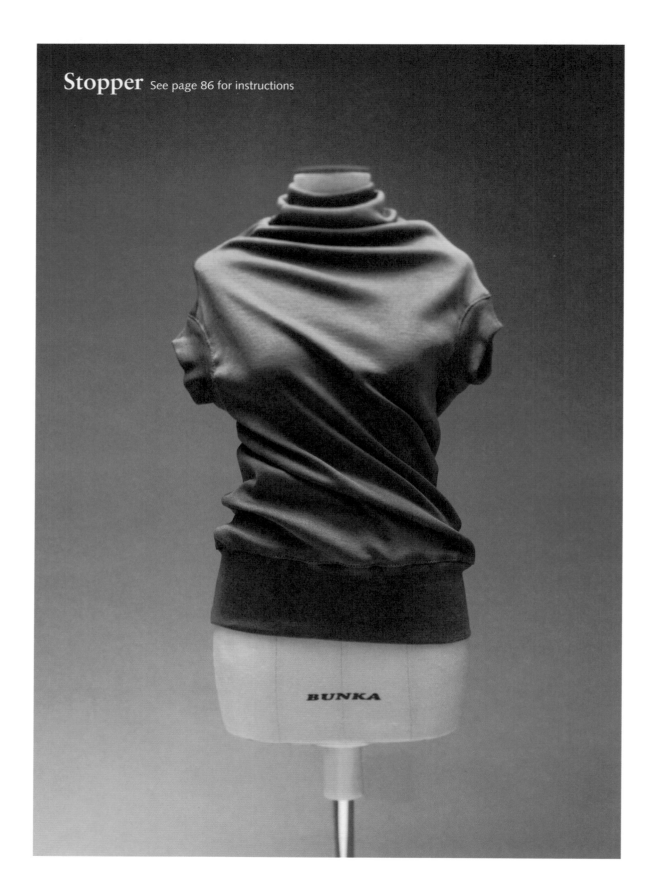

Loophole See pages 88 and 90 for instructions

B

A

63

Straight lines and curves A See page 93 for instructions

64
PATTERN MAGIC

Straight lines and curves B See page 94 for instructions

Kangaroo See page 96 for instructions

Stingray See page 100 for instructions

Making the patterns for
The expressive power of stretch fabrics

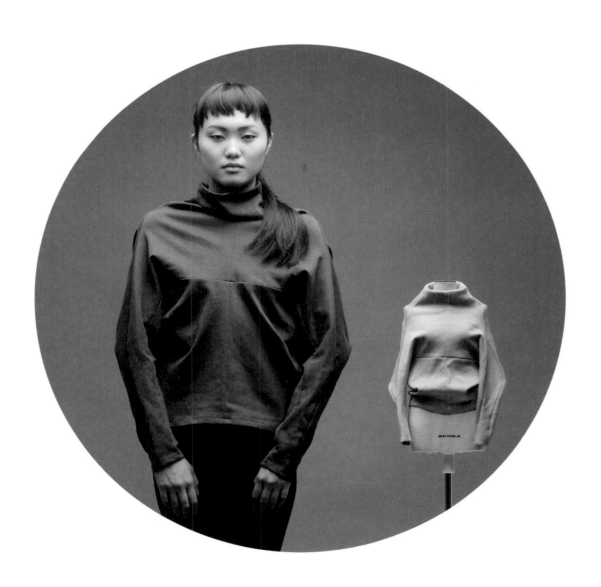

Page 49: Roots

Just as gradually unraveling a complex shape sometimes reveals a single, simple form, a simple shape can also take on many different guises. You could say the same about the process of making clothes, as your ideas evolve step by step into something fun that is more complex or sophisticated.

Here, we start with a barrel shape.

Roots sloper (block)

Roots A

Roots A

Roots B

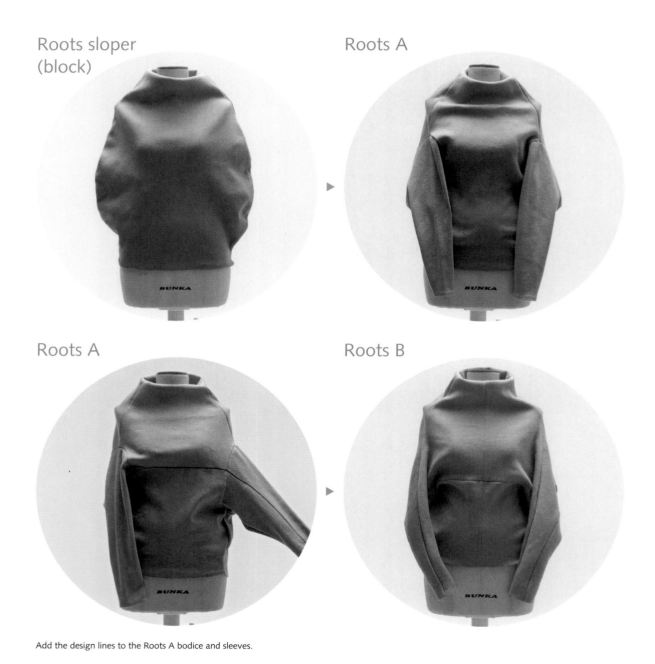

Add the design lines to the Roots A bodice and sleeves.

Roots sloper (block)

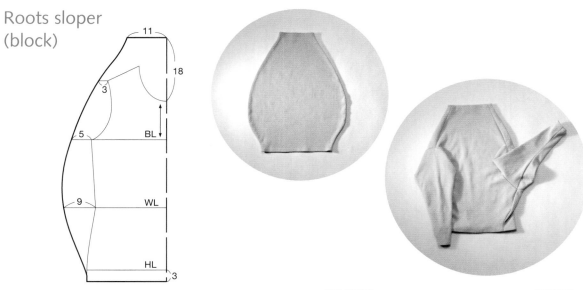

Draw up from the hip on the front sloper (block). The pattern will be made up of two sheets forming the front and back of the barrel shape.

Roots A

Add the shirt sleeves by moving the design lines on the sides horizontally. The sleeves attach right on the front, leaving the silhouette with bags of room at the back.

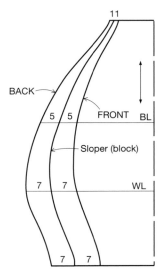

❶ Draw the Roots sloper (block). Move the design lines on the sides such that the front is on the inside and the back on the outside.

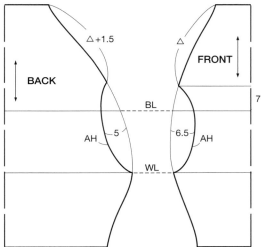

❷ Reverse the pattern to draw the back. Draw the arm holes up from the waistline.

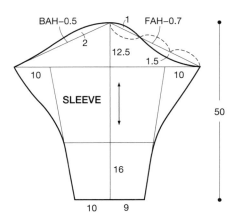

❸ Draw the pattern for the shirt sleeves. The sleeve caps will have the same measurements as the arm holes.

Roots B

Add the design lines along the sleeves from the Roots A bodice. Fold the bodice front so that it slouches forward. Add elbow bend shapes to the sleeves to give more of a turtle silhouette. Join the bodice and sleeves.

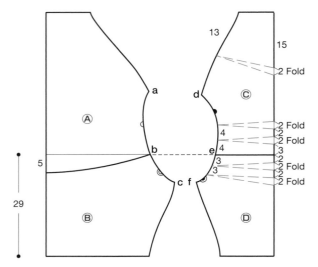

❶ Draw Roots A. Add the horizontal design lines, and divide the bodice front and back into Ⓐ, Ⓑ, Ⓒ, and Ⓓ. Fold over the center front to make the slouching silhouette.

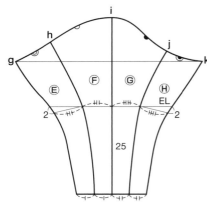

❷ Trace the arm hole measurements divided by the design lines onto the sleeve caps. Draw vertical design lines on the sleeves and divide the pattern into Ⓔ, Ⓕ, Ⓖ, and Ⓗ.

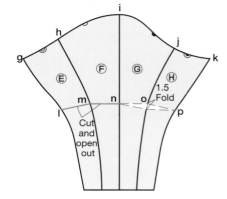

❸ Make the elbow bends on the elbow lines.

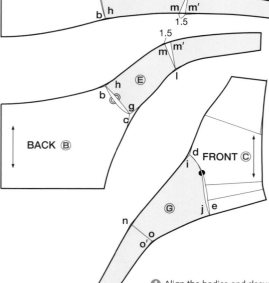

❹ Align the bodice and sleeves at the sleeve insertion position and draw smoothly and continuously.

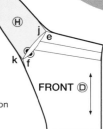

Page 50: Sharp and snappy A

I cut and opened out the pattern before adding
a single triangular spike.

As the dress form is being fitted with stretch material,
the spike appears to protrude sharply.

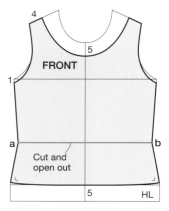

① Draw up from the hip line on the front sloper (block) to make the
pattern for the bodice. Draw the position of the incisions.

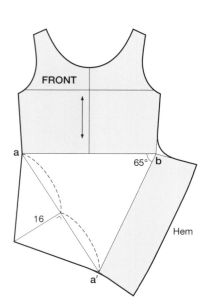

② Cut and open out at an angle of 65 degrees from reference point
b. Draw an isosceles triangle with a' as its base. This will form the spike
when the garment is worn.

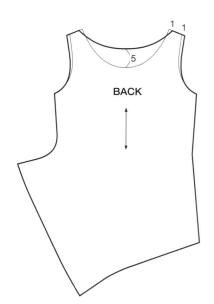

③ For the bodice back, reverse the front pattern made in ②.

Page 51: Sharp and snappy B

Try making two spikes on the right and one on the left.

By working with a rectangle, you can create two spikes at once so that, here, the rectangle and triangle together produced three spikes.

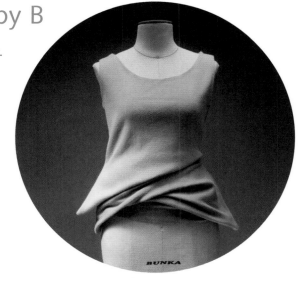

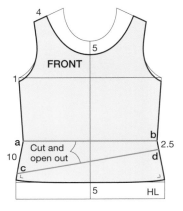

① Draw up from the hip line on the front sloper (block) to make the pattern for the bodice. Draw the position of the incisions.

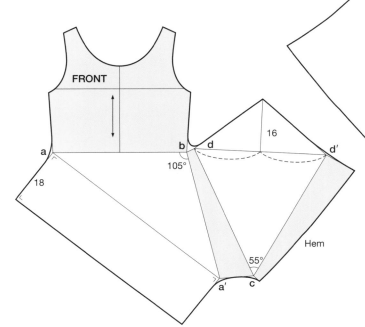

③ For the back, reverse the front pattern made in ②.

② Cut and open out at an angle of 105 degrees from reference point b. Draw a rectangle with a-a' as one side. Cut and open out at an angle of 55 degrees from reference point c. Draw an isosceles triangle with d-d' as its base. This will form the spike when the garment is worn.

Page 52: Sharp and snappy C

Make four spikes on each side.

This flares out the waist, producing a striking, tutu effect.

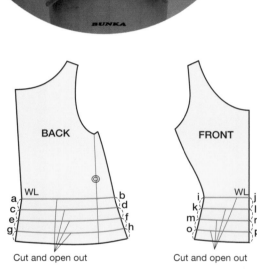

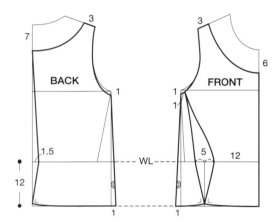

1 Draw up from the waistline on the back sloper (block) to make the bodice back pattern.

2 Draw up from the waistline on the front sloper to make a bodice front pattern with panel lines.

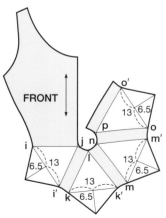

Cut and open out   Cut and open out

3 Align the front side with the bodice back. Draw the position of the incisions.

4 Draw the position of incisions on the bodice front too.

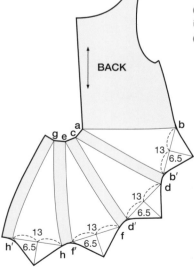

5 Make an opening of 13cm with a as the reference point. Draw an isosceles triangle with b-b' as its base. Cut and open out the remaining design lines in the same way.

6 Cut the front open in the same way.

Page 53: Sharp and snappy D

Here, we add a spike to the sleeves.

The result is a rather imposing, epaulette-like spike coming from the raglan sleeve.

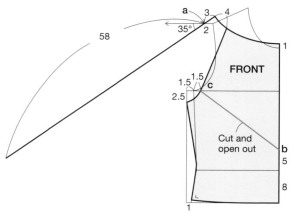

❶ Draw up from the waistline on the front sloper (block). Add a 35-degree diagonal at reference point a, determine the sleeve length, and draw the raglan lines. Draw the incision lines on the front.

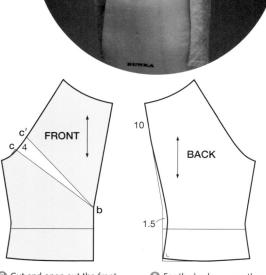

❷ Cut and open out the front and add some ease.

❸ For the back, reverse the front in ❷. Narrow the waist at the center back.

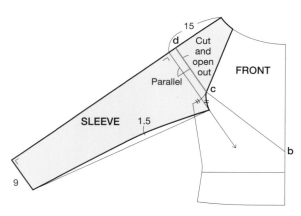

❹ Draw the sleeve pattern contiguous to ❶, drawing incision line c-d to match the ease in the bodice in ❷.

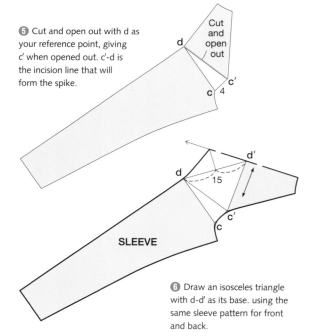

❺ Cut and open out with d as your reference point, giving c' when opened out. c'-d is the incision line that will form the spike.

❻ Draw an isosceles triangle with d-d' as its base. using the same sleeve pattern for front and back.

Page 54: Apple peel A

The skin of a wholly peeled apple curls into a helix shape.

Stretch it from both ends and the outside of the helix will gently ripple.

Let's try making sleeves in the form of an apple peel.

Insert plenty of design lines and cut in a circular motion like an apple peel.

The smaller the circles, the more of a ripple you'll achieve, and the rippled drape effect is multiplied when you put your arm through a round sleeve.

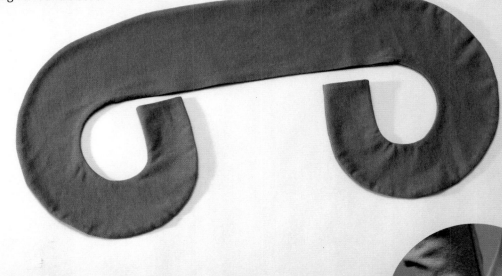

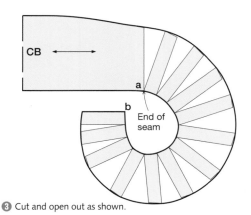

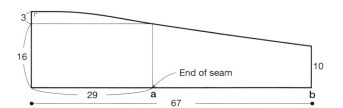

❶ Draw the pattern for the bolero. a-b will be the sleeve, but dont't make the seam on the curve too long because it will stretch.

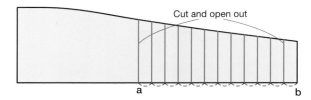

❷ Draw the incision lines.

❸ Cut and open out as shown.

Page 56: Apple peel B

The apple peel idea applied to a pair of pants (trousers) produced a snail shell pattern.

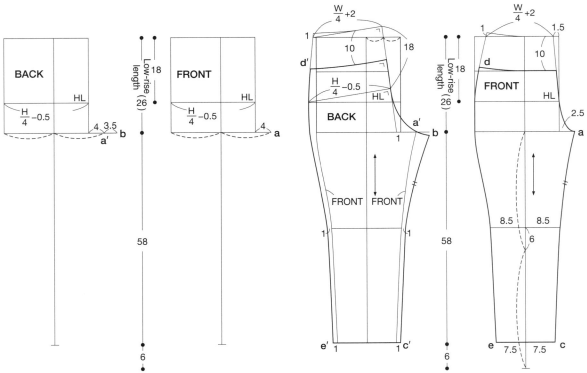

❶ Draw the base line of the trousers. Make the pants length short, as the pants will stretch once cut and opened out.

❷ Draw the patterns from the front. The waist is lowered by 10cm to allow for the low waist and the attachment of a belt.

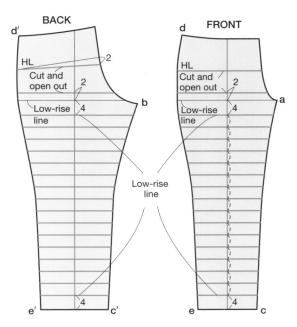

BACK

d'

HL

Cut and
open out

2

2

Low-rise
line

4

b

e'   4   c'

FRONT

d

HL

Cut and
open out

2

2

Low-rise
line

4

a

e   4   c

Low-rise
line

③ Draw the incision lines.

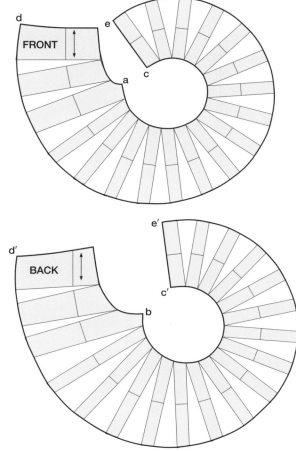

d

FRONT   ↕

e

a   c

d'

BACK   ↕

e'

c'

b

④ Cut and open out from the front. Make a similar circular cut and
opening for the back, as shown in the drawing, opening such that d-e
and d'-e' have the same measurement.

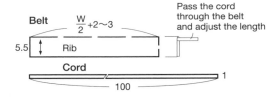

Belt $\frac{W}{2}+2\sim3$

5.5 ↕   Rib

Cord

100

1

Pass the cord
through the belt
and adjust the length

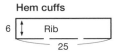

Hem cuffs

6 ↕   Rib

25

⑤ Draw the patterns for the belt, hem cuffs, and drawstring. Thread
the drawstring through the belt and adjust the length.

Page 58: Jutting edge

What kind of drape effect do you get by picking up a jutting edge and then letting it go?

How does a wide-bottomed conical shape like that of Mount Fuji translate into a pattern design?

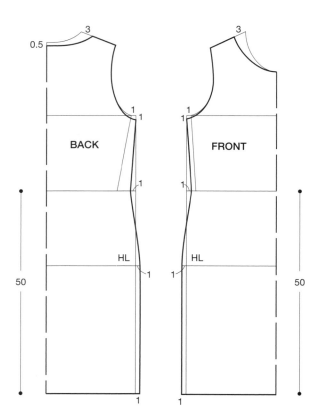

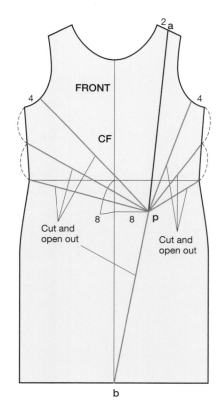

❶ Draw up from the waist on the front and back slopers (blocks). Draw the patterns for the front and back.

❷ Draw the design lines and incision lines on the bodice front, setting the position of the jutting edge as p. Cutting open with p as the reference point will give more height to the jutting effect, so place p at a relatively high position. a-p is the design line.

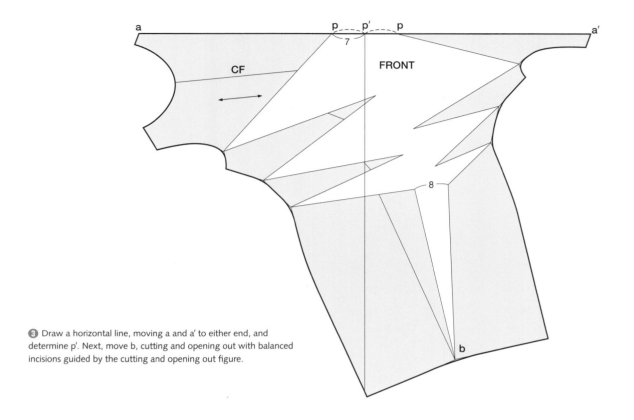

3 Draw a horizontal line, moving a and a' to either end, and determine p'. Next, move b, cutting and opening out with balanced incisions guided by the cutting and opening out figure.

Viewed from the side, the arm hole is created by a large, circular drape effect, reminiscent of the attire of Grecian gods. Between neckline and hem are lots of three-dimensional gathers, which are achieved with the careful addition of fine vertical stitching.

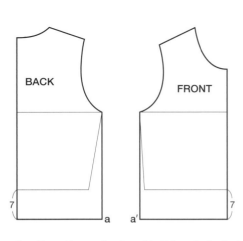

❶ Draw from the waist up on the sloper (block) to make the front and back patterns.

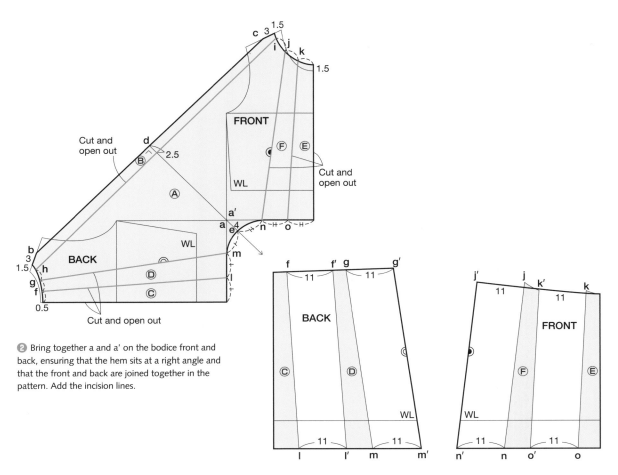

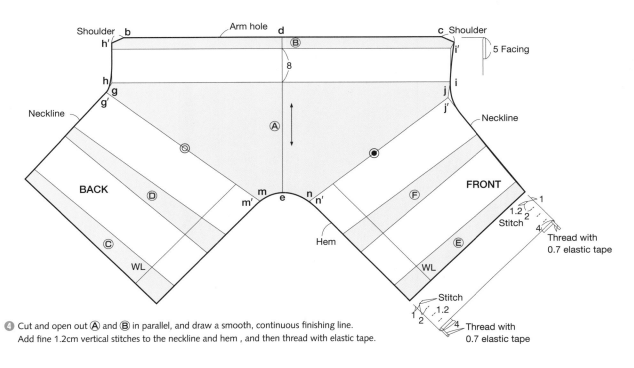

2 Bring together a and a' on the bodice front and back, ensuring that the hem sits at a right angle and that the front and back are joined together in the pattern. Add the incision lines.

3 Draw Ⓒ, Ⓓ, Ⓔ, and Ⓕ horizontally along the waist line.

4 Cut and open out Ⓐ and Ⓑ in parallel, and draw a smooth, continuous finishing line.
Add fine 1.2cm vertical stitches to the neckline and hem , and then thread with elastic tape.

Page 60: Stopper

Clothes with a twist in them will try to revert to their original form, which is why they need a stopper.

This top has twists going right the way from neck to hem, and the ribs on the neckline, arm holes, and hem help firm up the pretty drape effect.

The ribs also play a dual role as high-neck and sleeves.

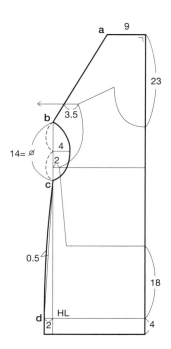

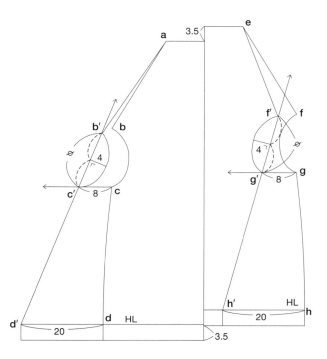

❶ Draw up from the waist on the front sloper (block). I have given the shirt some extra volume in order to add the twist.

❷ As we will be adding the twist from right to left, raise the left bodice by 3.5cm when drawing. Draw the right bodice pattern. Draw straight lines linking the points measured 20cm horizontally from d and 8cm horizontally from c, and move the arm hole. Draw the left bodice pattern. Draw straight lines linking the points measured 20cm horizontally from h and 8cm horizontally from g, and move the arm hole. This adds the twist to the pattern.

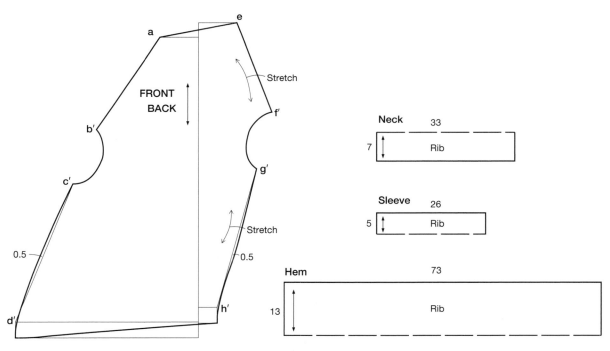

❸ Smoothly and continuously draw in the finishing line. Align the sides and shoulders at their longest section and then stretch and sew.

❹ Draw the patterns for the collar, sleeves, and hem.

Page 62: Loophole A

With stretch fabrics, even narrow loopholes widen out, allowing fabric to pass through them at will.

The same holes then try to return to their original size, barring the fabric's way and locking it in place.

This design is my attempt to make good use of design lines to make a loophole and the fabric that passes through it.

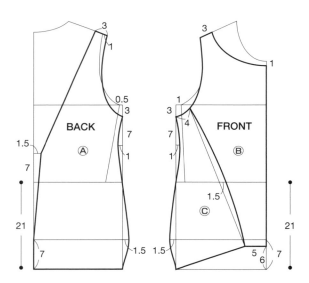

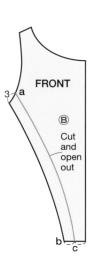

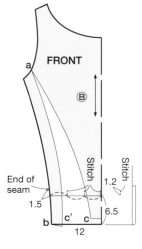

❶ Trace from the waist up on the front and back slopers (blocks). Draw the bodice front and back patterns as panels Ⓐ, Ⓑ, and Ⓒ.

❷ Draw the incision line on Ⓑ.

❸ Cut and open out with reference to a and draw the seam end. Add fine, 1.2-cm stitches perpendicular to the hole, because the area that forms the loophole will not be three dimensional if you make it into a tube with a single line of stitches.

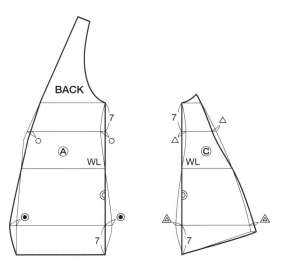

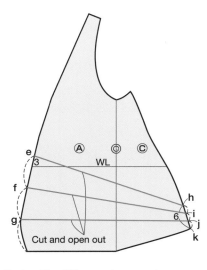

4️⃣ Adjust the lines on each side to straight lines in order to align the front and back sides into a single pattern, because the draped effect is prettier if there are no side seams.

5️⃣ Align Ⓐ and Ⓒ. Draw the incision lines.

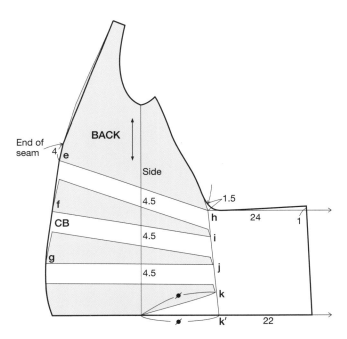

6️⃣ Cut and open out the incision lines in parallel. Draw the fabric that will pass through the loophole and smoothly and continuously draw the finishing line.

Page 62: Loophole B

The loophole is placed asymmetrically to give a modern feel.

I have dispensed with the side seams to produce a design that envelopes the waist in a single piece of material.

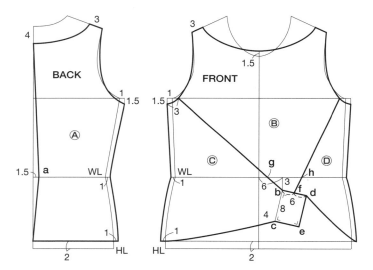

BACK

FRONT

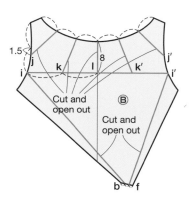

Cut and open out

Cut and open out

❶ Draw up from the hip line on the front and back slopers (blocks). Draw the pattern for the back. Draw the left and right of the front, naming the panels Ⓐ, Ⓑ, Ⓒ, and Ⓓ respectively. Draw the pattern for the loophole.

❷ Draw the incision line on Ⓑ.

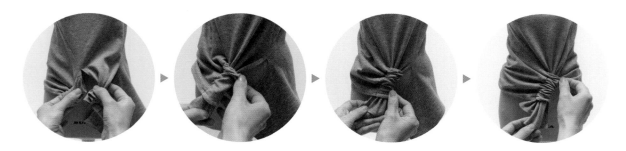

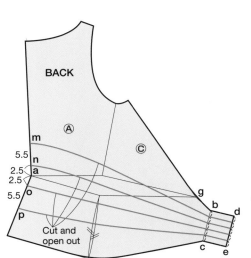

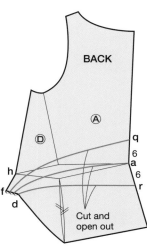

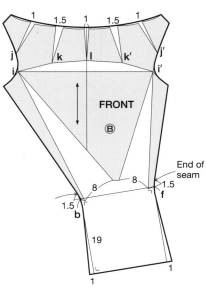

❸ Draw the right bodice pattern. Cut off at the waist line and align the sides. Align the top and bottom bodice panels at a and g. Draw the incision lines.

❹ Reverse Ⓐ and draw the pattern for the left bodice. Cut off at the waist line and align the sides. Align the top and bottom bodice panels at a and h. Draw the incision lines.

❺ Cut and open out Ⓑ. Draw the fabric that will pass through the loophole and finish smoothly and continuously.

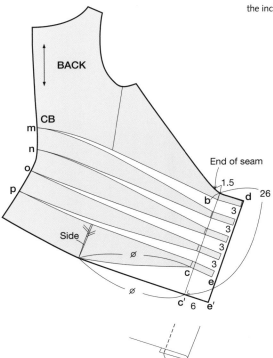

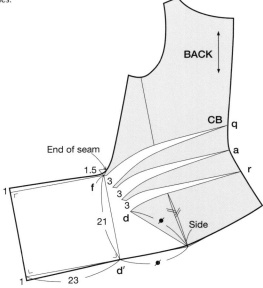

❼ Cut and open out the left bodice. Draw the pattern for the fabric that will pass through the loophole and smoothly and continuously draw the finishing line.

❻ Cut and open out the right bodice panel. Draw the seam end. Stitch to create the loophole.

Straight lines and curves

Straight lines and curves seamed together seem to breathe so much life into the fabric, it looks like it might spring into motion at any moment.

They can produce some wonderful three-dimensional shapes that far exceed the anticipated sum of their parts.

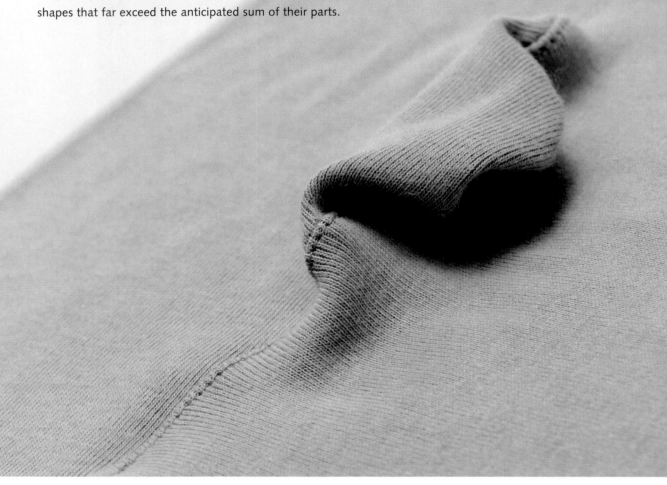

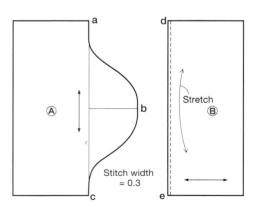

On curve Ⓐ, draw a, b, and c. On straight line Ⓑ, draw d and e.
Stretch d-e to the distance a-b-c, and sew together. It's easier to sew with Ⓑ underneath when you do this.
Fold the seam allowance back onto Ⓑ. Stitch with Ⓑ on top. Stitching allows you to keep the fabric in its stretched, sewn position.

Page 64: Straight lines and curves A

I've given the sleeves a substantial curve, like the humps on a camel's back, and made the bodice more compact so that the sleeves stand out.

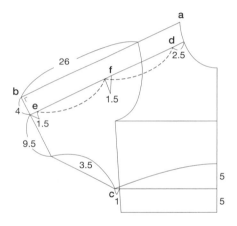

❶ Draw up from the waist on the front sloper (block). Draw the pattern for the bodice front.

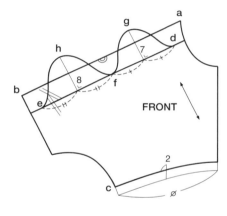

❷ Draw straight lines and curves on the shoulder design lines and add the hemline fabric.

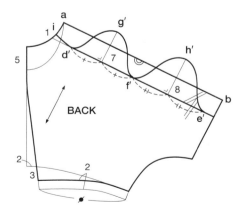

❸ Reverse ❶ and draw the pattern for the bodice back. Draw straight lines and curves on the shoulder design lines and add the hemline fabric.

❹ Align the front and back shoulders.

Stitch width = 0.3

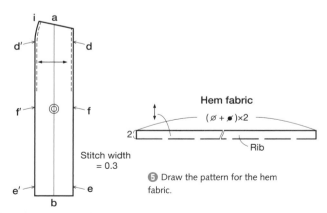

Hem fabric

$(\varnothing + \varnothing) \times 2$

Rib

❺ Draw the pattern for the hem fabric.

Page 65: Straight lines and curves B

Adding straight lines and curves to the shoulder blade region produces a garment that looks so beautiful from the back it is as if it has sprouted angel wings.

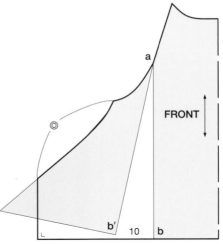

2 Cut and open out the bodice front. Smoothly and continuously draw the finishing line.

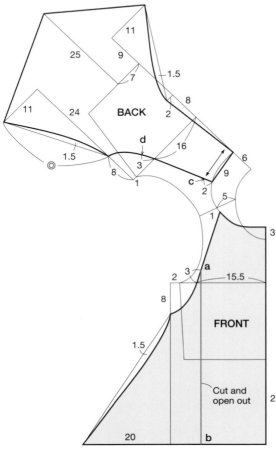

1 Align the front and back slopers (blocks) at the shoulders and draw. Draw the patterns for the bodice front and back. Insert the incision line on the bodice front.

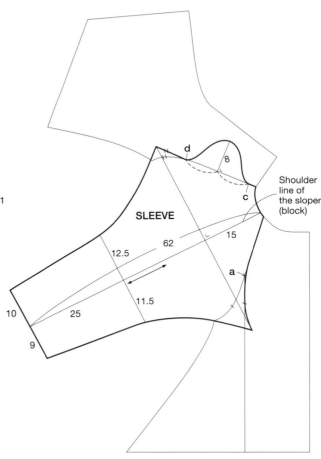

3 Draw the sleeve pattern over the pattern in **1**. Draw the curve on the back raglan line. Smoothly and continuously draw the finishing line.

Page 66: Kangaroo

A top with large round pouches like a kangaroo's.

Bringing in the drawstring attached at the center front makes the
pouches puff out into rounder shapes, while the head appears
almost to wriggle free from the slits in the back.

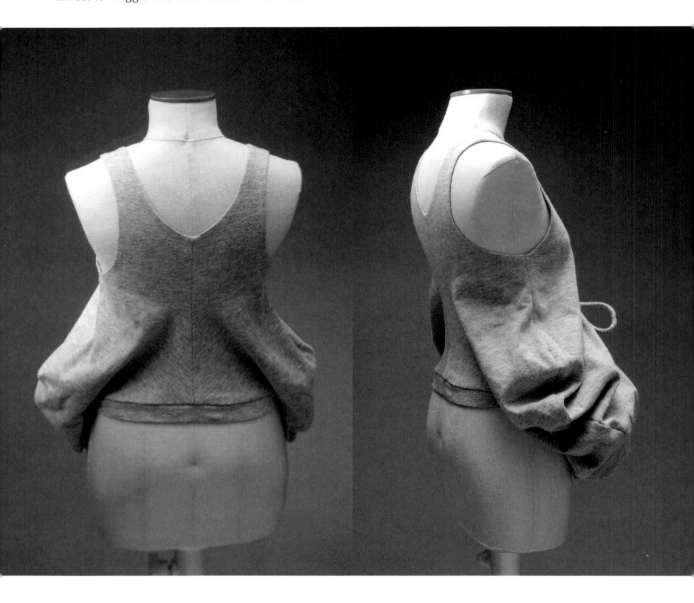

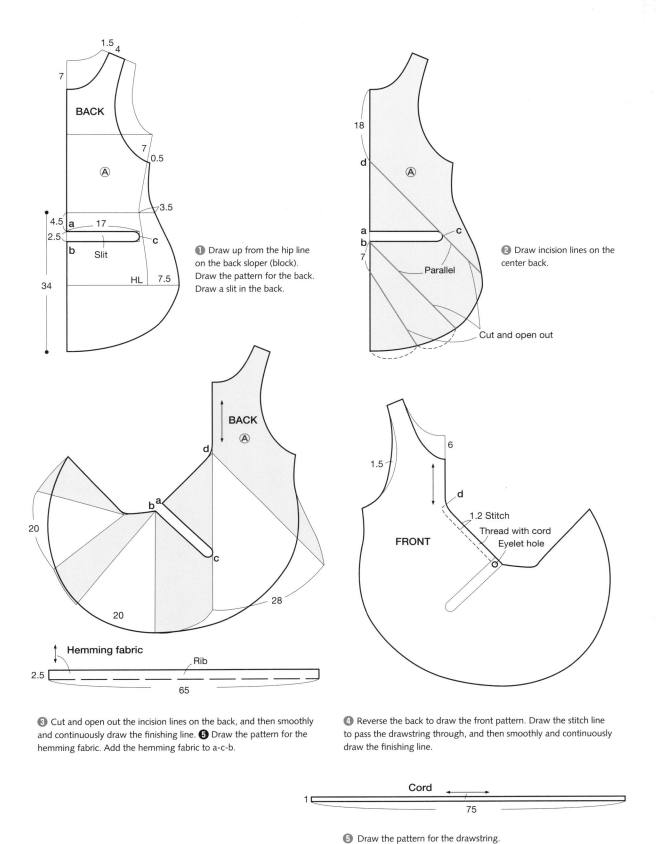

BACK

Ⓐ

1.5 4

7

7

0.5

3.5

4.5 a   17

2.5

b   Slit   c

34

HL   7.5

❶ Draw up from the hip line on the back sloper (block). Draw the pattern for the back. Draw a slit in the back.

18

d

Ⓐ

a   c

b

7

Parallel

Cut and open out

❷ Draw incision lines on the center back.

BACK

Ⓐ

d

b a

c

20

20

28

Hemming fabric

Rib

2.5

65

6

1.5

d

1.2 Stitch

Thread with cord

Eyelet hole

FRONT

o

❸ Cut and open out the incision lines on the back, and then smoothly and continuously draw the finishing line. ❺ Draw the pattern for the hemming fabric. Add the hemming fabric to a-c-b.

❹ Reverse the back to draw the front pattern. Draw the stitch line to pass the drawstring through, and then smoothly and continuously draw the finishing line.

Cord

1

75

❺ Draw the pattern for the drawstring.

Page 68: Stingray

A popular feature of aquariums, the stingray is a sight to behold as it heads towards you flapping its fins widely, yet there's something rather adorable about its demure face, of which we're given a fleeting glimpse as it turns to show its underbelly.

Anyhow, the outspread skirt and flattened in-profile silhouette somehow remind me of that creature in the aquarium.

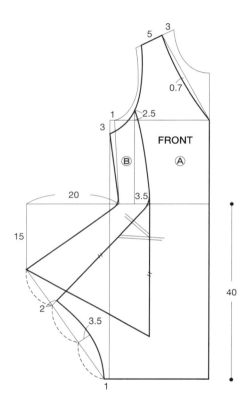

❶ Draw up from the waist on the front sloper (block). Draw the pattern for the front. Draw the panel lines, intersecting the panel lines spreading out at the sides to create a pattern for a skirt with a draped effect.

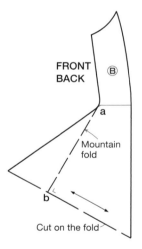

❷ Cut the sides on the fold at the hem to create a pattern in which front and back are contiguous. Create a mountain fold (shown by a dash-dot line) on a-b to give three dimensional space to the sides.

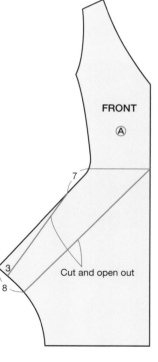

❸ Draw the incision lines on the center front bodice.

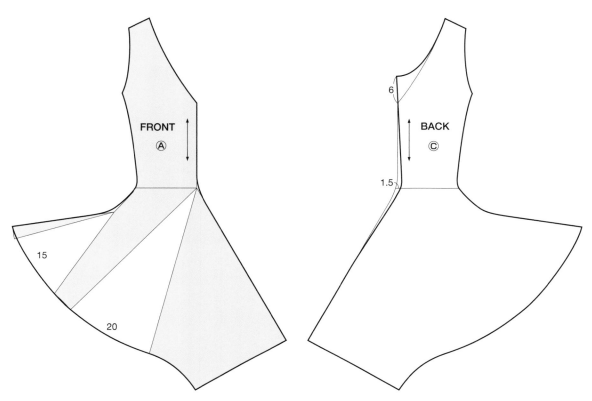

4 Cut and open out the incision lines on the center front panel. Smoothly and continuously draw the finishing line.

5 Reverse the center front panel to draw the pattern for the bodice back. Narrow by 1.5cm at the waist line. Raise the neckline by 6cm at the center back. Smoothly and continuously draw the finishing line.

Enlarging and reducing patterns

Patterns can be enlarged and reduced with a photocopier, but you can also do it by working out the proportions.

By way of example, we'll expand the "Two peas in a pod" pattern on page 32 to 135% and reduce it to 65%.

Expand to 135%

Reduce to 65%

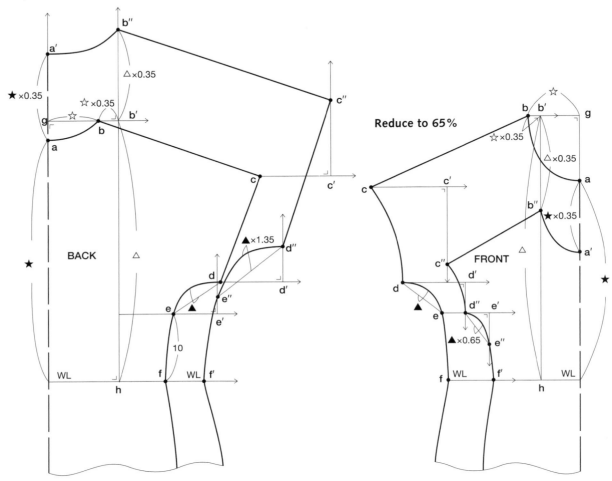

① Draw the back. Draw points a, b, c, d, e, and f. Enlarge horizontally to 135% with reference to the center back. Draw g at a right angle from b on the center back. Draw a horizontal line from g through b. Measure g-b as the distance ☆. Measure (☆ × 0.35) from b, calling the point b'. Measure 35% of the length from the center back to c horizontally from c in the same way, and call the point c', and then measure d', e', and f' using the same approach. Repeat the process for the area below the waist. Enlarge vertically to 135% with reference to the waist. Mark the measurement from a to the waist on the center back as ★. Measure (★ × 0.35) from a and call the point a'. On the waistline, measure h at a right angle to b'. Draw a vertical line from h through b'. Call the distance from b' to h measurement △. Measure (△ × 0.35) from b', calling the point b'', and then measure c'', d'', and e'' in the same way. Enlarge the area below the waist upwards. To draw the neckline curve, connect d-e, and call the deepest point on the curve measurement ▲. Connect d''-e'', measure the distance (▲ × 1.35), and draw the curve. Draw the neckline curve in the same way, working smoothly and continuously through the new points that you have created.

② Draw the front. Draw points a, b, c, d, e, and f. Reduce horizontally to 65% with reference to the center front. Draw g at a right angle from b at the center front. Connect b-g. Measure g-b as the distance ☆. Measure (☆ × 0.35) from b, calling the point b'. and then measure c', d', e', and f' using the same approach. Repeat the process for the area below the waist. Reduce vertically to 65% with reference to the waist. Mark the measurement from a to the waist on the center front as ★. Measure (★ × 0.35) from a and call the point a'. On the waistline, measure h at a right angle to b'. Connect b'-h. Call the distance from b' to h measurement △. Measure (△ × 0.35) from b', calling the point b'', and then measure c'', d'', and e'' in the same way. Reduce the area below the waist upwards. To draw the neckline curve, connect d-e, and call the deepest point on the curve measurement ▲. Connect d''-e'', measure the distance (▲ × 0.65), and draw the curve. Draw the neckline and cuffs in the same way, working smoothly and continuously through the new points that you have created.

Finished pattern

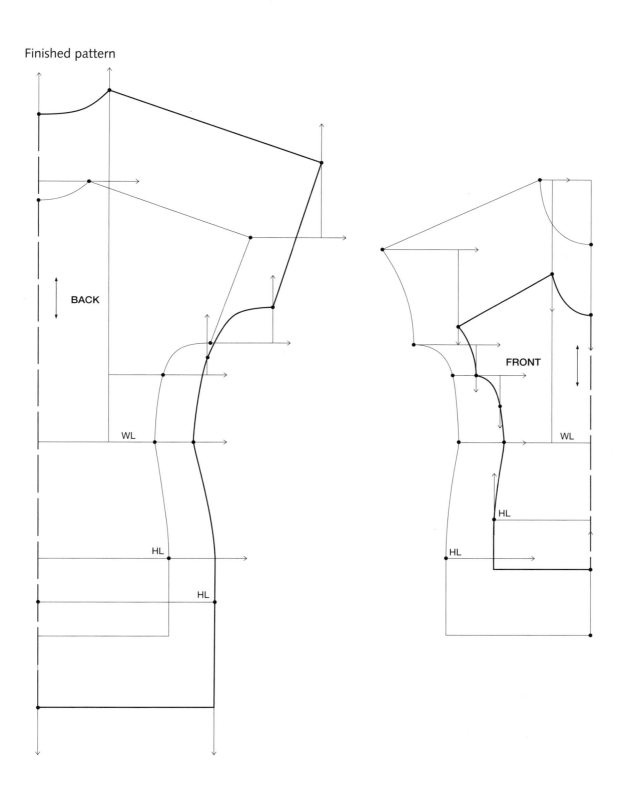

BACK

WL

HL

HL

FRONT

WL

HL

HL

In conclusion

Stretch fabrics are the closest we have to the skin we were born with.

They say that it was Coco Chanel who, prompted by the scarcities of wartime, first put the jersey fabrics once used solely for underwear to work in outer garments, and I'm sure it was the flexibility of the material that made it so comfortable.

And then there was Madeleine Vionnet, who in the absence of stretch fabrics would use the soft texture of fabric cut on the bias to give her clothing that same softness of expression.

Wonderfully versatile, stretch fabrics are all about the enjoyment of making garments 'outside the box', from inspiration, and they might well come to your rescue if you're puzzled as to how to make something.

Pattern Magic has now reached its third volume, and as with the previous two, I'd like to express my thanks to Fujino Kasai and the many other people who have given their support.